MW00720387

© 2002 by Barbour Publishing, Inc.

ISBN 1-58660-459-7

Cover image © Getty One

Scripture quotations are taken from the King James Version of the Bible.

Published by Barbour Books, an imprint of Barbour Publishing, Inc., P.O. Box 719, Uhrichsville, Ohio 44683, www.barbourbooks.com

 Member of the
Evangelical Christian
Publishers Association

Printed in China.
5 4 3 2 1

# To Have and to Hold

RACHEL QUILLIN

DayMaker
GREETING BOOKS

To have and to hold

From this day forward

For better, for worse,

For richer, for poorer,

In sickness and in health,

To love and to cherish,

Till death us do part.

*Dear Bride and Groom,*

Today you celebrate your love for one another. Let this be true all the days of your lives. As the traditional wedding vows say, you have one another to hold "from this day forward"—in every situation. Share each other's joys and sorrows. Love one another regardless of your financial status, as love is one of the greatest riches you can have. Stand by each other in illness, and rejoice with one another in health. Cherish each other until your last day on earth.

Above all, let your relationship to your heavenly Groom reign paramount. After all, marriage is a beautiful union, especially when God is at the center. A good marriage has been described as a triangle with God being the top point and the husband and wife each at one of the other points. As the husband and wife move toward God, they also move closer to one another. Pray together and for each other. Share God's Word together, and learn to love Him more together. Then you will draw closer to Him and closer to one another.

May He bless you as you begin your life together!

Hope is like a harebell, trembling from its birth;
Love is like a rose, the joy of all the earth;
Faith is like a lily, lifted high and white;
Love is like a lovely rose, the world's delight.
Harebells and sweet lilies show a thornless growth,
But the rose with all its thorns excels them both.

CHRISTINA ROSSETTI

And now abideth faith, hope, charity, these three;

but the greatest of these is charity.

1 CORINTHIANS 13:13

$K$nit your hearts with an unslipping knot.

WILLIAM SHAKESPEARE

$C$*hains do not hold a marriage together.*
*It is threads, hundreds of tiny threads*
*that sew people together through the years.*

SIMONE SIGNORET

$M$arriage resembles a pair of shears,
so joined they cannot be separated;
often moving in opposite directions,
yet always punishing anyone who comes between them.

SYDNEY SMITH

*Life is the flower of which love is the honey.*

VICTOR HUGO

*Love is the fairest bloom in God's garden.*

UNKNOWN

*Love is a mixture of honey and bitterness.*

CISTERELLA

*H*ear the mellow wedding bells,—
Golden bells!
What a world of happiness their harmony foretells!
Through the balmy air of night
How they ring out their delight!
From the molten golden notes,
What a liquid ditty floats
To the turtle-dove that listens, while she gloats
On the moon!
Oh from out the sounding cells,
What a gush of euphony voluminously wells!
How it swells!
How it dwells
Oh the Future! How it tells
Of the rapture that impels
To the swinging and the ringing
Of the bells, bells, bells. . .
To the rhyming and the chiming of the bells!

EDGAR ALLAN POE,
from "The Bells"

# Savior Like a Shepherd Lead Us

Savior, like a shepherd lead us, much we need Thy tender care;
In Thy pleasant pastures feed us, for our use Thy folds prepare.
Blessed Jesus, blessed Jesus! Thou hast bought us, Thine we are.
Blessed Jesus, blessed Jesus! Thou hast bought us, Thine we are.

Early let us seek Thy favor, early let us do Thy will;
Blessed Lord and only Savior, with Thy love our bosoms fill.
Blessed Jesus, blessed Jesus! Thou hast loved us, love us still.
Blessed Jesus, blessed Jesus! Thou hast loved us, love us still.

*Love is not like a reservoir. You'll never drain it dry.*
*It's much more like a natural spring.*
*The longer and farther it flows,*
*the stronger and the deeper and the clearer it becomes.*

EDDIE CANTOR

Plant a word of love heart-deep. . . .
Nurture it with a smile and a prayer,
and watch what happens.

MAX LUCADO

*Dear heavenly Father,*
*thank You for the love that You have given us.*
*Help it to grow stronger and more precious every day.*
*Amen.*

*A successful marriage requires*
*falling in love many times,*
*always with the same person.*

MIGNON MCLAUGHLIN

Happy marriages begin when we marry the ones we love,
and they blossom when we love the ones we marry.

TOM MULLEN

*It is not your love that sustains the marriage,*
*but from now on, the marriage that sustains your love.*

DIETRICH BONHOEFFER

$\mathcal{L}$ove is, above all,
the gift of oneself.

JEAN ANOUILH

$\mathcal{T}$here is nothing so loyal as love.

ALICE CARY

$\mathcal{A}$ wise lover values not so much
the gift of the lover
as the love of the giver.

THOMAS À KEMPIS

*M*arried life offers no panacea—
if it is going to reach its potential,
it will require an all-out investment by
both husband and wife.

JAMES C. DOBSON

*W*ives, submit yourselves unto your own husbands,
*as unto the Lord.*
*Husbands, love your wives,*
*even as Christ also loved the church,*
*and gave himself for it.*

EPHESIANS 5:22, 25

*He* who loves something mentions it very often.

ARABIAN PROVERB

*I love you, not because you are perfect,*

*but because you are so perfect for me.*

UNKNOWN

*Immature* love says:
"I love you because I need you."
Mature love says:
"I need you because I love you."

ERICH FROMM

*P*ut on therefore, as the elect of God, holy and beloved, bowels of mercies, kindness, humbleness of mind, meekness, longsuffering;

Forbearing one another, and forgiving one another, if any man have a quarrel against any: even as Christ forgave you, so also do ye.

And above all these things put on charity, which is the bond of perfectness.

And let the peace of God rule in your hearts, to the which also ye are called in one body; and be ye thankful.

Let the word of Christ dwell in you richly in all wisdom; teaching and admonishing one another in psalms and hymns and spiritual songs, singing with grace in your hearts to the Lord.

And whatsoever ye do in word or deed, do all in the name of the Lord Jesus, giving thanks to God and the Father by him.

Wives, submit yourselves unto your own husbands, as it is fit in the Lord.

Husbands, love your wives, and be not bitter against them.

COLOSSIANS 3:12–19

*Where we love is home,*
*home that our feet may leave,*
*but not our hearts.*

WENDALL HOLMES

*I* am my beloved's,
and my beloved is mine.

SONG OF SOLOMON 6:3

*Never forget that the*
*most powerful force on earth is love.*

NELSON ROCKEFELLER

# The Beauty of Love

The question is asked, "Is there anything more beautiful in life than a young couple clasping hands and pure hearts in the path of marriage? Can there be anything more beautiful than young love?"

And the answer is given. "Yes, there is a more beautiful thing. It is the spectacle of an old man and an old woman finishing their journey together on that path. Their hands are gnarled, but still clasped; their faces are seamed, but still radiant; their hearts are physically bowed and tired, but still strong with love and devotion for one another. Yes, there is a more beautiful thing than young love. Old love."

ANONYMOUS

*Love does not consist in gazing at each other*

*but in looking together in the same direction.*

ANTOINE DE SAINT-EXUPÉRY

*T*he goal in marriage is not to think alike,
but to think together.

ROBERT C. DODDS

*Love is an action, an activity.*

*It is not a feeling.*

M. SCOTT PECK

# A Happy Home Recipe

*Serves: Many*

| | |
|---|---|
| 4 cups of love | 5 spoonfuls of hope |
| 2 cups of loyalty | 2 spoonfuls of tenderness |
| 2 spoonfuls of kindness | 3 spoonfuls of understanding |
| 3 cups of forgiveness | 4 quarts of faith |
| 1 cup of friendship | 1 barrel of laughter |

Take love, loyalty, and forgiveness; mix thoroughly with faith. Blend with tenderness, understanding, and kindness. Add friendship and hope; sprinkle abundantly with laughter. Bake with sunshine. Serve daily.

$\mathcal{L}$ove comforteth
like sunshine after rain.

WILLIAM SHAKESPEARE

$\mathcal{L}$*ove is a great beautifier.*

LOUISA MAY ALCOTT

$\mathcal{L}$ove builds bridges
where there are none.

R. H. DELANEY

*Live joyfully with the wife whom thou lovest
all the days of the life.*

ECCLESIASTES 9:9

*T*he secret to a long marriage is
to put a little romance in every day.

UNKNOWN

*The development of a really good marriage
is not a natural process.
It is an achievement.*

DAVID AND VERA MACE

*I*ntimacy. . .
the mystical bond of
friendship, commitment, and understanding.

JAMES C. DOBSON

*Love is a symbol of eternity.*
*It wipes out all sense of time,*
*destroying all memory of a beginning and all fear of an end.*

ANNE-LOUISE-GERMAINE DE STAËL

*H*e's more myself than I am. Whatever our souls are made of, his and mine are the same. . . . If all else perished and he remained, I should still continue to be, and if all else remained, and he were annihilated, the universe would turn a mite stranger. . . . He's always, always in my mind; not as a pleasure to myself, but as my own being.

EMILY BRONTË, *Wuthering Heights*

Marriage is not finding that person
with whom you can live,
but finding that person
with whom you cannot live without.

HOWARD HENDRICKS

Dear Lord Jesus,
thank You for marriage.
Please let the union of our lives be a picture of
the marriage of Christ to the Church.
Help us to seek the best for one another
and to love each other always and unconditionally.
Amen.

*L*ove alone is capable of uniting human beings
in such a way as to complete and fulfill them,
for it alone takes them and joins them
by what is deepest in themselves.

PIÉRRE TEILHARD DE CHARDIN

*O love, resistless in thy might,*

*thou triumphest even over gold!*

SOPHOCLES

*A*nd walk in love, as Christ also hath loved us,
and hath given himself for us
an offering and a sacrifice to God
for a sweetsmelling savour.

EPHESIANS 5:2

*Accept*
*the secret of a good marriage*

**A**ttraction

**C**ommunication

**C**ommitment

**E**njoyment

**P**urpose

**T**rust

ANONYMOUS

*W*hen we reflect on the meaning of love,
we see that it is to the heart what summer is
to the farmer's year.
It brings to harvest
all the loveliest flowers of the soul.

BILLY GRAHAM

*Behold, thou art fair, my love;*

*behold, thou art fair.*

SONG OF SOLOMON 4:1

*O*my Luve's like a red, red rose.

ROBERT BURNS

$\mathcal{T}$herefore shall a man leave his father and his mother,
and shall cleave unto his wife:
and they shall be one flesh.

GENESIS 2:24

*$\mathcal{L}$et the wife make her husband glad to come home,
and let him make her sorry to see him leave.*

MARTIN LUTHER

$\mathcal{M}$arriage is that relation between man and woman
in which the independence is equal,
the dependence mutual, and the obligation reciprocal.

LOUIS K. ANSPACHER

*Love gives itself; it is not bought.*

HENRY WADSWORTH LONGFELLOW

*L*ove is not an affectionate feeling,
but a steady wish for the loved person's ultimate good
as far as it can be obtained.

C. S. LEWIS

*Love is the greatest gift*

*a person can give another.*

# O Perfect Love

O perfect Love, all human thought transcending,
Lowly we kneel in prayer before Thy throne,
That theirs may be the love which knows no ending,
Whom Thou forevermore dost join in one.

O perfect Life, be Thou their full assurance,
Of tender charity and steadfast faith,
Of patient hope and quiet, brave endurance,
With childlike trust that fears nor pain nor death.

Grant them the joy which brightens earthly sorrow;
Grant them the peace which calms all earthly strife,
And to life's day the glorious unknown morrow
That dawns upon eternal love and life.

Love is something so divine,

Description would but make it less;

'Tis what I feel, but can't define,

'Tis what I know, but can't express.

BEILBY PORTEUS

*Wherefore they are no more twain, but one flesh.*
*What therefore God hath joined together,*
*let not man put asunder.*

MATTHEW 19:6

Marriage has in it less of beauty,
but more of safety, than the single life;
it has more care, but less danger;
it is more merry, and more sad;
it is fuller of sorrows, and fuller of joys;
it lies under more burdens,
but it is supported by
all the strengths of love, and charity,
and those burdens are delightful.

JEREMY TAYLOR ·

*H*ow do I love thee?
Let me count the ways. . . .
If God choose,
I shall but love thee better after death.

ELIZABETH BARRETT BROWNING

*Love is not, then, primarily a matter of emotions.*
*It is a commitment of the will. God wills to love us,*
*come what may. . . .*
*To fall in love under God is*
*to share this quality with one's partner.*

LIONEL A. WHISTON

*E*xcept the LORD build the house,
they labour in vain that build it.

PSALM 127:1

*A happy marriage is the union of two good forgivers.*

ROBERT QUILLEN

Now you will feel no rain
for each of you will be shelter for the other;
Now you will feel no cold
for each of you will be warmth for the other;
Now there is no more loneliness
for each of you will be companion for the other;
Now you are two bodies
but there is only one life before you;
Go now to your dwelling place
to enter into the days of your togetherness,
And may your days be good and long upon the earth.

NATIVE AMERICAN BLESSING

*My heart is ever at your service.*

WILLIAM SHAKESPEARE

*N*o cord or cable can draw so forcibly,
or bind so fast,
as love can do with a single thread.

ROBERT BURTON

*Where love reigns,
the very joy of heaven itself is felt.*

HANNAH HURNARD

*There is nothing more admirable than two people
who see eye-to-eye keeping house as man and wife,
confounding their enemies, and delighting their friends.*

HOMER

You ought to trust me for I do not love and will never love any woman in the world but you, and my chief desire is to link myself to you week by week by bonds which shall ever become more intimate and profound.

Beloved I kiss your memory—your sweetness and beauty have cast a glory upon my life.

SIR WINSTON CHURCHILL,
to his wife Clementine

*L*ove is like a friendship caught on fire.
In the beginning a flame, very pretty,
often hot and fierce but still only light and flickering.
As love grows older, our hearts mature,
and our love becomes as coals,
deep burning and unquenchable.

BRUCE LEE

*The heart that loves is always young.*

UNKNOWN

*L*ove makes those young whom age doth chill,
And whom he finds young, keeps young still.

PETER CARTRIGHT

The Christian is supposed to love his neighbor,
and since his wife is his nearest neighbor,
she should be his deepest love.

MARTIN LUTHER

*Intreat me not to leave thee,*
*or to return from following after thee:*
*for whither thou goest, I will go;*
*and where thou lodgest, I will lodge:*
*thy people shall be my people, and thy God my God:*
*Where thou diest, will I die,*
*and there will I be buried:*
*the LORD do so to me, and more also,*
*if ought but death part thee and me.*

RUTH 1:16–17

$\mathcal{L}$ove is a great thing, a great and thorough good; by itself it makes everything that is heavy light; and it bears evenly all that is uneven.

It carries a burden which is no burden; it will not be kept back by anything low and mean; it desires to be free from all worldly affections, and not to be entangled by any outward prosperity, or by any adversity subdued.

Love feels no burden, thinks nothing of trouble, attempts what is above its strength, pleads no excuse of impossibility.

It is therefore able to undertake all things, and it completes many things, and warrants them to take effect, where he who does not love would faint and lie down.

Though weary, it is not tired; though pressed, it is not straitened; though alarmed, it is not confounded; but as a living flame it forces its way upward, and securely passes through all.

Love is active and sincere; courageous, patient, faithful, and prudent.

THOMAS À KEMPIS

*The LORD bless thee, and keep thee:*
*The LORD make his face shine upon thee,*
*and be gracious unto thee:*
*The LORD lift up his countenance upon thee,*
*and give thee peace.*

NUMBERS 6:24–26

As you commit your lives this day to one another, I pray that you will also commit your lives to seek and do the will of God together, for it is in His will that His greatest blessings are found.

*May God go with you as you pledge yourselves to*

*"have and to hold"*

*each other from this day forward.*